VICKY RODEN

MS. RODEN'S
COMPENDIUM
OF THE
FANTASTICAL
&
MYTHOLOGICAL
FROM ANCIENT TIMES TO THE MODERN DAY

VICKY RODEN

ISBN: 1489547428
ISBN-13: 978-1489547422

In gratitude for the types of stories that are loved
not wisely, but too well.

CONTENTS

ACKNOWLEDGMENTS

The Author gratefully acknowledges the assistance of the Broadwoodwidger Museum of Cryptozoology and Mythology in the research of this Compendium, together with the support and fraternity of Mr. Ian Messenger, Mr. Thomas Smith and all those beyond counting who've encouraged me in my efforts.

Thank you all for making the Monsters Wager.

INTRODUCTION

I began writing this compendium to celebrate obscure mythologies – the oddities which one sees occasionally referenced in history books, as an old tale told by a mad aunt, or as the lonely, yet lovely, odd exhibit in municipal museums. During my research I was tremendously lucky to be able to spend an extended period of research at the Broadwoodwidger Museum in Liskeard and was astounded by the fellowship and enthusiasm this institution, and the ancient family who still maintain it, had for my project.

The museum and staff have produced a sister publication to this compendium, extracts of which they have graciously allowed me to print alongside this all too slim edition. It is a lifetime's work to achieve what I wish to achieve, and as such this is the first edition of what I hope will be a constantly evolving work.

Not forgetting the miracles of the modern age the information in these pages is also available online at www.rodenscompendium.wordpress.com – one of my abiding memories of my time at the museum is the joyous abandon with which the staff opened their treasured libraries and storerooms to me, with the same attitude of sharing of information that made the Viscount of Broadwoodwidger more concerned with preserving his collection of knowledge rather than his family name back in the Napoleonic era. In this way I seek to return the favour, and encourage others to do the same.

The Hon. Cecelia Amhurst, current head of the board of trustees at the Broadwoodwidger Museum, suggested that this Compendium also contain some modern mythologies as seen in the worlds of fantasy, science fiction and computer games. These are some of our most important burgeoning folk stories, and while formats change the need of humanity for fantasy and distraction remains as consistent as ever. However, this is an area which requires a whole compendium of its own. They are also, like dragons and unicorns, vastly represented elsewhere, particularly online, and this work is very much intended to highlight some rather more obscure mythologies.

While some of the entries are a few lines, there are others, such as the mythology of Nonny Warn, which have become more in depth studies. I hope this work will encourage the discovery and preservation of stories, mythologies and fantasies that are the spice of life.

Vicky Roden

THE COMPANION TO THE COMPENDIUM

EXTRACTS FROM THE BROADWOODWIDGER PUBLICATION

A Note from Dr. J.J. Smallman, Director of the
Broadwoodwidger Museum

It is with genuine pleasure that I present 'A Companion
to the Compendium', presented as an accompanying
volume to the upcoming 'Ms Roden's Compendium of
the Fantastical and Mythological' that was partially
researched at the museum and includes several items
from our collection.

The Broadwoodwidger Museum was established in 1807
when Charlton Amhurst, the sixth Viscount of
Broadwoodwidger, set off to fight in the Napoleonic
Wars. A renowned collector of curiosities, Fellow of the
Miskatonic University and bachelor, he sought to ensure
the preservation of his collection and continuation of his
research by establishing the museum at his town
lodgings in Liskeard and bestowing a healthy
endowment to fund its ongoing maintenance. Over the
next few years the institution attracted visitors and
researchers from across the country, and upon his return
he was so impressed by the reputation the museum had
gained that he established it as a more permanent centre
for the research of the mythological and public display
of unusual and inexplicable objects. As such we present
here several essays deliberating on the natures and
notions of Myth and Fantasy, including new work from
several figures associated with the museum including
the Dean of the Faculty of Comparative Mythology at
the Miskatonic University in Massachusetts, an
establishment with which we have enjoyed a long and
fruitful relationship and where Charlton Amhurst
elected to study in his youth, eschewing the traditional
institutions open to him and electing to travel to the

colonies to continue studies in his area of interest.

Since the establishment of the museum mankind has altered considerably – at the time of opening the industrial revolution was in full swing, and since then the world has seen the advent of mechanisation, mass transport, compulsory education, several worldwide conflicts, space travel, and finally the computer age. As a museum of cryptozoology (the study of creatures of doubtful existence) and mythology (the study of doubtful histories) we have seen our specialism come in and out of fashion and have occasionally expected there to come a day when these studies are no longer relevant to mankind. This day has never come. If anything the proliferation of information now available to humanity has made our position more relevant, our continued work more valuable, as mythology and fantasy touch upon more aspects of society. To this end we have sought, in this publication, to define what these subjects mean in the modern era, how they manifest themselves and also discuss their importance to society.

For over two centuries we have gladly received and investigated such objects that defied categorisation elsewhere, and we intend this to continue for several centuries to come!

THE FANTASTICAL

"**fantastic** *adj* **1a** unreal or imaginary. **b** so extreme as to challenge belief; incredible. **2** marked by extravagant fantasy or eccentricity; unrealistic. **3** (informal) wonderful; eccentric. **>> fantastical** *adj…*"

As defined in the Penguin Dictionary c. 2007

The Functions of Fantasy

Ada Rosemarther, Lecturer in Regressive Psychology & Parapsychology, St Jude's .

Unlike the myth, with its is-it-isn't-it potential for a basis in reality, the fantastic refuses to be limited to so mundane a concept as truth. Fantasies are wild, fantasies are weird, and done correctly fantasies can change the world for the better!

Fantasy is also tremendously honest – it has no need to hide behind a veil of possibility. It does not require explanation nor does it need acceptance. It simply is, and our attitude towards it leads to the word 'fantastic' being used as a compliment, whereas referring to something as 'mythical' suggests (even at a subconscious level) deceit and lies. The fantastic suggest the new, the creative, progression, whereas the mythical smacks of adherence to old ideas long since misunderstood and misinterpreted. Fantasy also leads to the potential for future reality, whereas the mythical leads inevitably to the misnomers of the past.

Unlike mythology, which often functions as a means to justify horrors committed in the names of belief, fantasy (save a few individual acts of violence) serves to encourage thought and questioning, leading often to cultural and scientific breakthroughs. Chiefly among these are the fantasies surrounding science fiction, from the writings of Jules Verne to the gaudy camp of Star Trek. While much maligned by critics such feats of imagination are instrumental in attaining feats of scientific achievement, inspiring the invention of the submarine, helicopter and mobile telephone among many others.

Some of these inventions directly reference the fantasy that spawned them – the Taser, a well-known non-lethal weapon, derives its name from Victor Appleton's 1911 book Tom Swift and his Electric Rifle and is an acronym of "Thomas A. Swift's Electric Rifle" with inventor John Cover being inspired by the stories of his childhood. Science fiction writing also inspired Philip Rosendale's development of online gaming community 'Second Life', with him acknowledging Neil Stephenson's 1992 novel Snow Crash as a major influence on his long held ambition to create the online community by "…painting a compelling picture of what such a world could look like in the near future…".

Second Life continues to gather a million users worldwide into a single virtual community, concerts are staged there, land is bought and homes are built there, and artists create work there. One such artist is China's Cao Fei who represented her country simultaneously at the 2007 Venice Biennial and on Second Life via her avatar China Tracy. Fei created a digital installation in Venice and a China Tracy pavilion online which was described as "…an adventure into this virtual world that is exerting crucial influence on our perception of the real…".

The installation was the digital made real, being an inflatable building in the manner of the associated online 'Moon Garden' where the both the physical and online audiences could interact and merge. Fei continued working on Second Life with her RMB City project, creating a virtual city of Chinese landmarks and culture from the Birds Nest Olympic stadium to Tiananmen Square, and invited others to join and build in her city. She was later to observe how, despite the virtual environment, avatars were very often indicative of a users personality and that social conventions, such as personal space, are still practiced. She also notes how there is a tendency for people to attempt to resolve real world problems and compensate for perceived shortcomings through this medium, and seems dubious about the value of such forms of catharsis.

However, I feel that this illustrates one of the functions of fantasy – to allow us a safe place to work out such issues, to resolve and diffuse uncomfortable feelings before they affect our real world relationships. Computer games, from the massive social network of Second Life to personal console titles, can have an immensely positive impact on those who play them, with many examples discussing the usefulness of games in overcoming bereavement, loss and in providing a means to engage with the world when suffering depression. One gamer describes how, following the death of her father, a game managed to engage her and provide the right analogy to help her move on "My player in the game, …still had missions to do, people to save. Life could go on … because things had to be done." There are scores of similar tales, and whereas in the past a grieving person might seek consolation from a religious figure, soothsayer or medium these testimonials show that such fantasies are perfectly capable of fulfilling the same function.

Fantasy is once of the finest mental tools possessed by

man, and one of the most important for humanity's continued evolution. For besides the surface benefits of fantasy as a means of entertainment and diversion, there is also the pervasiveness of its influence. Fantasy is singular in that it inspires both art and science, and everything in between – the only function of a fantasy is to exist as an idea, and as such the means by which it can be interpreted and extended are limitless.

THE MYTHOLOGICAL

"**mythological** *adj* **1** relating to or dealt with in mythology or myths. **2** lacking factual or historical basis."

As defined in the Penguin Dictionary c. 2007

THE MYTH IN THE MODERN ERA

PROF. C.H. FREELOVE, DEAN OF THE FACULTY OF
COMPARATIVE MYTHOLOGY, MISKATONIC UNIVERSITY,
ARKHAM, MASS.

We are a funny little species. Each of us lauding over our
ancestors while being equally susceptible to the same
tricks, certain that our 'technologies' and world
weariness set us an evolutionary notch above our
hundredth great grandparents, who still trembled at the
thoughts of the demonic and the holy. Such enlightened
creatures we!

While it IS true that we are less susceptible to the notion
of sun gods and fairies, we are still as dependant on the
myth and the fantastic as ever – more so, now that that
cold of the winter and unfavourable weather conditions
can be explained away without recourse to angered
deities. In dedicating his work on deific mythology to
Douglas Adams Richard Dawkins quoted the question
"Isn't it enough to see a garden is beautiful without
having to believe that there are fairies at the bottom of it
too?", but it is the beauty of the garden that makes us
fantasise about what creatures may dwell in such a
place. Very few pixies frolic on cold hard patio slabs,
and the elfkind rarely linger among the decrepit
mattresses and plastic bags that often decorate urban
'green' spaces such as canal banks. But the urge to
fantasise remains unchecked by either evolution or
education, and a good thing too! For now we can take
charge of our mythologies and shape them for our own
entertainment and ends, rather than using them to
assuage the fears of the dark and cold, or explain why

13

the moon waxes and wanes. The focus of mythology shifts.

In this time of the miraculous-made-commonplace we have, rather like those ancestors who wove the mythology of faith into their crop planting and wood chopping, given ourselves the opportunity to add a healthy dose of fancy to almost every aspect of our daily lives. For those in need of a hero to worship there are a myriad of musicians, actors, and public figures to extend ones devotion to, for those wishing to play the hero there are social media sites galore where your history is as you want it to be, and for those wishing to immerse themselves more fully in a land of fantasy you can assume the identity of a huge variety of creatures (human, orc, elf or extra-terrestrial) and interact in countless settings (faraway lands, post-apocalyptic futures and humanity's own past) through the mediums of TV, cinema and computer games. However, these myths are less about the rationalisation of that which we do not understand, and more about the joy of life. We can dismiss much of what is unknown with a blithe 'There's some scientific reason for it', but the need for myth, its functions and its uses remain as relevant as ever. The Jungian idea of mythology gives it the attributes of an interpreter between the conscious and the unconscious mind and a personification of the world beyond man. Jung noted the progression of myths through mans technological development considering that, rather than creating mythologies that connected this individual to a world beyond its ken, modern man sought instead to re-establish a sense of connection from this vast, impersonal world back to the internally experienced one. Yet mans development of myth continues itself to evolve, with mythologies seeking to link inner world to inner world via the interconnectivity of the digital age and the assiduously interactive formats of the fan convention. Mythology continues to allow us to anthropomorphasise and connect to these unknown planes, and to engage with those who also share some aspect of our history.

A convention simply means a gathering of people for a specific goal or cause, and while the ease and anonymity of online communities can be said to be part of its popularity the convention marks its polar opposite where the digital construct is made real. A recent addition to the regular convention circuit is that of Costumed Play, or Cosplay, whose attendees often spend large amounts of time transforming themselves into favourite characters from various modern mythologies, in particular films and computer games, and bringing together thousands of people in one location to trade thoughts and celebrate their shared passions. Is there really much difference between the elaborate, home made costumes worn proudly at Cosplay conventions and the elaborate costumes worn by players acting out the eddas and sagas? By being able to dress as these fantasy characters, the cosplayers are imbibing these computerised, or mechanical, figures with human physicality, reclaiming them from the 'external' world as part of their personal mythology in much the same way as performers of old would invoke their gods through dramatic renderings.

Re-Making the Mythical

J.J Smallman, director

Mythology and mankind develop with one another – that is to say that, as mankind continues to exist it not only refines and expands on its existing folklores but also develops new mythologies based on the needs of the current generation.

Culture seems to constantly devour itself. As we become aware not only of our own histories, but of the histories of cultures across the world, our myths and legends are being re-written and re-presented to echo our modern sensibilities. Whereas in the nineteenth century we were introduced to the mythologies of other cultures (leading to highly romantic notions about them, and the lionisation of those explorers who pillaged these seemingly 'primitive' people in order to have interesting objects to display and discuss at high tea) the twenty-first century seeks to re-discover their mythologies by re creating them.

For example, the popular American TV series 'Supernatural' deals with assorted monsters, beasts, gods and demons, spanning across the entirety of human history and culture. Each episode follows a fairly standard format and is in itself a modern variant of the hero saga, a pair of brothers travel across America in search of their missing father, hunting mythical beasts, monsters, solving paranormal riddles, fighting to overcome evil and generally prevailing. As such the show not only defines existing mythologies but also invites these mythologies into the modern era, giving such characters as the Trickster (a character who has featured in human folk tales since pre-history) the opportunity to wreak havoc in the modern day.

Another example of the myth re-written by popular culture is the Stargate franchise, which includes several films and television shows. However rather than taking a seemingly encyclopaedic approach to the mythologies it discusses Stargate appropriates mainly ancient legends, particularly the tales of the Gods of ancient Egypt, as being inspired by the actions of a powerful race of aliens who had once enslaved mankind. Here the theories of Gods-as-spacemen popularised by Erich von Daniken are given full licence to appear and show us their true natures. Both shows are rewriting mythology, with one using its format to create an entire bestiary of vampires, werewolves, pagan deities and cursed objects and the other using one primary source to create its own fables from.

Together with the recycling of the stories of our ancestors, we also willingly partake in new myths of a more modern age. One of the most obvious examples of these is the conspiracy theory. The first of these began in the late 1940's and often related to flying saucers and visitors from another world, but there are such stories debating such diverse topics as the incongruities of the moon landing, the reality of natural disasters and secretive organisations seeking world domination. Like traditional mythology it is passed by word of mouth or its modern equivalent, the Internet forum, from person to person and claims to explain the inexplicable or unbelievable. It also presents itself as being based, however tenuously, in fact. There are many who take

17

such claims as seriously as others take religious beliefs, and when such claims have become unfashionable they are looked upon with the same incredulity we now have for claims that the sun is delivered every morning by chariot.

Another common form of modern mythmaking is those who mythologise their own existence or find their actions mythologised by others. Celebrity, although not a new concept, has certainly become far more prevalent since the advent of the moving image, television and finally the Internet, where seemingly anybody can become famous at random and overnight. Art and the media have plenty of those who create their own mythological figures, including musicians such as David Bowie who would create vast back stories for his on-stage persona, Madonna who routinely alters her appearance, aesthetic and attitude, Andy Warhol and Salvador Dali who lived as their own, semi mythical creations and artists such as Spartacus Chetwynd who create fantastical mythologies as the focus of their work.

Much of the recent work in the exploration of mythology has come from the field of art, and the aforementioned Chetwynd's appropriation of her first name makes an interesting example of this. By taking the name of a hero, and a slave hero at that, Chetwynd instantly adopts the power and ethos of her namesake much like a berserker warrior donning a bearskin. By invoking the character by name she causes the audience to consider their response to the legend of Spartacus and extrapolate how this name could relate to her.

Continuing with the subject of the power of names,

David Bowie has made a career of creating mythologies around himself and his public persona. 'Ziggy Stardust' 'Major Tom' and 'The Thin White Duke' were all distinct characters with their own histories, and Bowie knew that in order to embellish these creations with the kernel of authenticity myth requires he must adequately play the part, from the trappings of fame such as excessive hotels and entourages to the lavish and extravagant concerts he played.

This approach has led to Bowie describing himself as feeling "more like an actor than a rock musician" and David Buckley describing him as "…supremely 'mythogenic'…" before going on to say "…it's the myth that has far greater resonance and is far more intriguing…".

For myths ARE intriguing – when we hear so many names every day it is the ones who have been mythologised that stand out – the name Andy Warhol conjures up the excesses of the Factory, the music of the Velvet Underground, endless screen printed images of movie stars and food packages. To say Einstein sparks images of wild white hair and the mysteries of the universe reduced to a single mathematical phrase, and the word 'Dali' has come to signify melted clocks and eccentric moustaches. Not that this is any kind of exhaustive list of these men's attributes, but is indicative of the mythologies attributed to each of them. The facts are somewhat irrelevant, and cumbersome, as Roland Barthes pointed out about the depictions of Einstein:

> "*photographs* of Einstein show him standing next to a blackboard covered with mathematical

signs of obvious complexity; but *cartoons* of Einstein (the sign that he has become a legend) show him chalk still in hand, and having just written on an empty blackboard... the magic formula of the world."

For this represents how humans mythologise. We refine our scientists down to their most singular achievements, literature down to its most immediate quotes, art down to its seminal works. We sacrifice the complexity of Einstein's blackboard, like Barthes's cartoonist, at the altar of mythology to create a super-human figure capable of plucking such mysteries from the ether.

For if a necessary mythology never existed or is no longer relevant, mankind will create or re-create it as necessary. We still seek guidance on examples of what is good, and what is heroic. Myth displays only the exemplary.

A Note on Compendium Entries

In order to ensure readers get the best experience of the compendium we here discuss the format of a compendium entry;

Section One: Names And Aliases

This section deals entirely with how an entity, object or event is referred to, both popularly and technically.

Section Two: Manifestations

The manifestation of an entry discusses its physical appearance or parameters – in the case of a creature it will discuss height, weight, appearance and such other reportable observations that can be discussed. In the case of an object it will include dimensions, description, and usual or natural location and in respect of an event it includes dates, locations, length of time and associated occurrences.

Section Three: Known Actions and Attributes

Actions and attributes refer to the non-physical markers of an entity, object or event. For example, the Hope diamond has a tendency to finish off any who hold it, but manifests itself as a large gemstone. A Coney Mock will appear playful and timid immediately prior to an onslaught, or if caught in isolation, but manifests itself as a long limbed, grey furred, human faced creature.

Section Four: See Also

A suggestion of related topics related to the entry.

CRYPTIDS AND CREATURES

THE CONEY MOCK

A.K.A: The Mock Coney, The Rabbit Snake, Monkey Dragon, The Grey Swarm, Tiny Siren

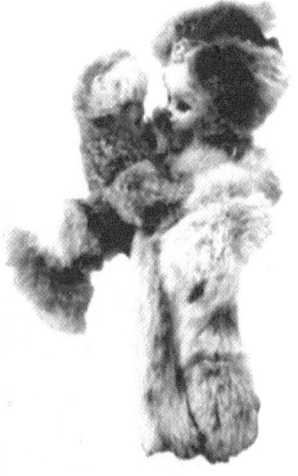

The Coney mock is a lithe figure, ostensibly humanoid and ranging in length from six inches to three feet. They have a grey fur, similar to a rabbit, which becomes thick and long on the head with a smooth face, much like a monkey but with more cat like features. In isolation they are shy and playful, often endearing themselves to visitors, but in larger numbers they swarm their enemies and use their long and flexible limbs to crack their victim's skull.

Usually this is one of the larger animals, such as wild pigs, that the Coney Mocks hunt in packs. In 1904 the Opogo-Bunyip expedition fell foul of these creatures.

According to the expedition notes of a young gentleman taking a far-flung journey to impress his fiancée the creatures appeared shortly after he and the rest of the crew stopped at an apparently uncharted island to explore. On the first night '..a pair of creatures seemed to gambol around the camp, and at once I had the thought that these would make the perfect engagement present for my Jenny'. He captured the creatures and caged them, intending to take them with him. The ship's captain, Erasmus Haniver, warned him against such actions to no avail.

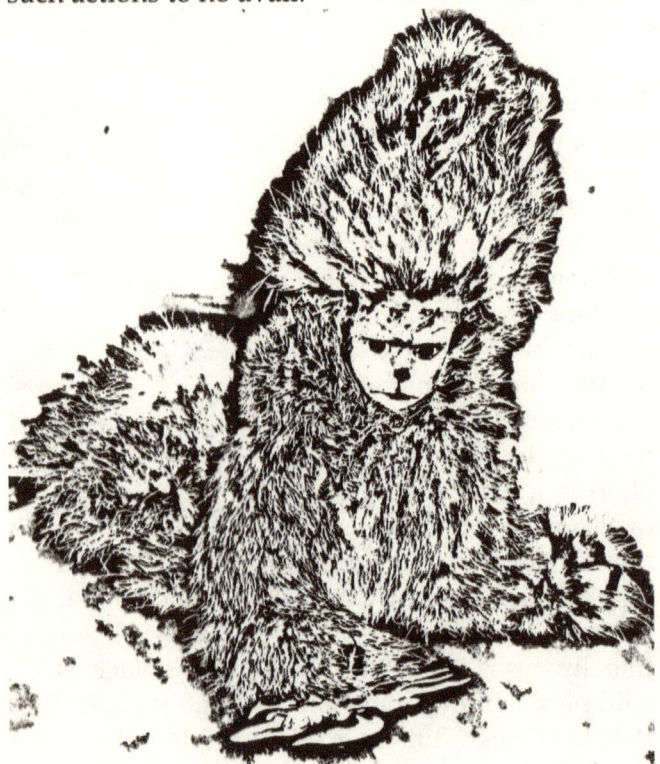

That night, shortly before dawn, the camp was swarmed by seemingly hundreds of the creatures, which killed or mortally wounded over half the crew, including the ships doctor. The rest escaped, and subsequent dissection of the Coney Mocks revealed it to consist not of bones but of wholly of cartilage and ligaments, accounting for it's incredible flexibility. '…the animals seemed able to twist themselves around the necks of the men, more like a snake than a legged creature.' The young gentleman and the Captain managed to escape to the ship with the caged Coney Mocks, and he did indeed present them to his fiancée. She, however, would have preferred a ruby, and the engagement faltered soon after.

The only known pair in captivity were last seen in the collection of curiosities of 'Haniver and Son'.

See Also: Haniver & Son.

THE DANCING ANGEL

A.K.A: Luna C. Fur, The fallen dancer.

There are several classes of Angel in Judeo-

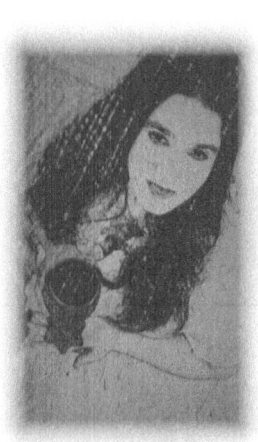

Christian Mythology, one host of which is charged with observing humanity. This myth concerns one who, usually concealed in moonbeams, became obsessed with the human practice of dancing. This particular angel eventually chose to eschew her heavenly role in order to experience dancing first hand, with her actions then leading to the demonisation of dance, particularly during the middle ages, as being an action that can make an Angel fall from Grace.

The tale of Luna was referred to in *Nonny Warn's further Tales*:

There one was a heavenly body it seems,
weaving her way among the moon beams
sent to observe the strange habits of man
which is how the story of Luna began.

She followed her wards with an interest so keen
she wondered if what she had seen was a dream
the acts of these creatures left her entranced,
particularly when they danced

For centuries it seemed she longed
to join the spinning, weaving throng
But to do such a thing was hardly the norm
and needed a solid, corporeal form

eventually the need grew too great
and once decided could barely wait
to set feet on that solid ground
and finally join the dancing crowd

She found it much finer than she thought
how it felt to frolic and cavort,
She Waltzed and Rumbaed, jigged and reeled,
Mastered the cha-cha and the quadrille

So now she dances, unable to stop
on this day she flounces, on that day she bops
for when she dances she feels joy abound
with no equal on heaven or earth to be found.

THE FROZEN MOLE

A.K.A: Barty

A small, grey, mole emerging from a clear surface.

The frozen mole was one of Shelley Smith Industries early experiments with metaphysical engineering. After finding some obscure texts on portals and their uses, Mr. Shelley Smith did a variety of experiments involving creating small portals and using them to transmit messages and images between each other. He then moved on to sending small objects through.

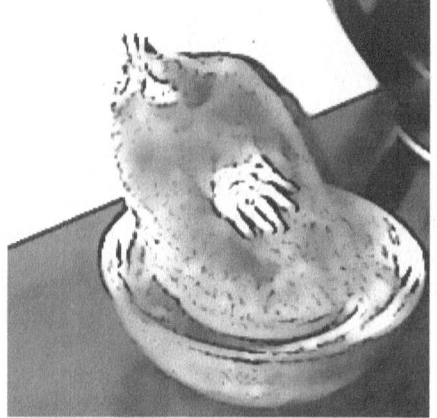

He discovered that dropping objects onto the portal led to them simply sitting on the surface, but actually pushing an item through the aperture pushed it out of the corresponding portal. Encouraged by this, he decided to do his first experiments with live subjects. The nearest critter he had to hand was his pet mole, Bartrum. He considered the Mole, with it's digging claws and sleek fur, to be the most suitable creature to pull itself through the portal and arrive safely on the other side.

Barty's entry went exactly as expected, but his return to reality was far from smooth. He appeared to be frozen, half in and half out, and seemed dead apart from his attitude and the warmth of his fur. Over the past hundred years approximately half of Barty's remainder has emerged, leading to speculation as to why the phenomenon occurred. The most popular theory is that the portal was miscast, and the temporal loop that usually protects the user from trans-dimensional shear was amplified, slowing Barty's movements to the point of inertia.

This was certainly Shelley-Smith's theory, and his heartbreak at the loss of his favourite pet led to his abandonment of the Portal Project.

Is has been suggested that Shelley Smith's notes have since been sent to Aperture Science, but that is currently speculative.

See Also: Shelley Smith Industries

THE GRINNING AXEMAN

A.K.A: The Happy Killer, The Chipper Chopper, The DreamGuard

A tall, grinning man who appears only in dreams, carrying a large, bloodied axe.

"As a child I was plagued by nightmares, then another terrifying figure emerged – a tall, broad man with manic hair, staring eyes a fixed grin and a huge axe with blood dripping off it. He scared me so much I'd immediately awake whenever I dreamed about him. But after a few weeks I noticed I was having less nightmares, although those that I did have always ended with the appearance of this grinning monster of a man.

I thought I'd just grown out of the night terrors, until one night I dreamed I was walking down a long red, corridor, and the Axeman was there, but sitting, with his weapon on the ground beside him. further along the corridor I could see the fallen forms of 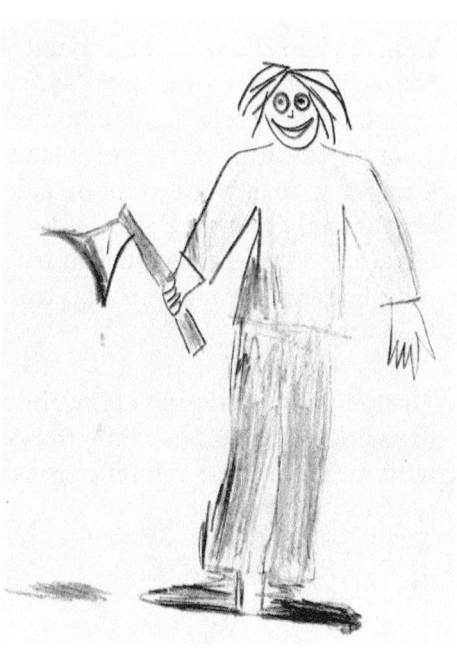 the giant Spiders, evil clowns and other childish things that had been the subjects of my nightmares before. So I walked up to the axeman, who looked at me with that horrible, twisted face, but I'd never before been close enough to him to see his eyes, which seemed so peaceful and brown. I realised that his fearsome appearance was not to frighten me, but to scare the real monsters that had kept me from sleeping for so long. I smiled at him, he patted my head and I woke up"

The Grinning Axeman is essentially a psychological barrier, but while studying sleep disorders and night terrors Dr. Rosemarther discovered several children had dreamed of a character with the same characteristics – a huge man with a fixed grin, armed with a perpetually bloodied axe, who always appeared at the conclusion of a nightmare and never, in a single account, actually acted aggressively toward the dreamer. She collected examples from across the country, and even found the character in dream studies from Germany, the USA and Japan.

The question of how so many children dreamt of the same character, fulfilling the same functions but without an obvious reference in waking life, remains unanswered.

MUTANT HELIANTHUS

A.K.A: Red Velvet

A large sunflower with a prominent single eye.

The question of the possibility of sentience in plants has been around for as long as there have been minds to inquire of it. There are countless tales, reports and speculations, but the appearance of the Mutant Helianthus seems to have confirmed that sentience is not restricted to animal life.

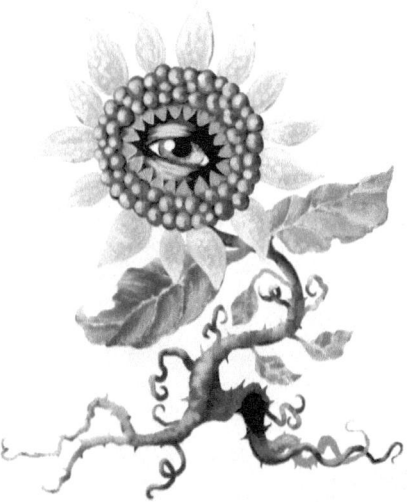

Artist and botanist Marit Cooper recalled in a radio interview how she first discovered this extraordinary specimen, which she affectionately calls 'Red Velvet';

"It has recently transpired that the Mutant Helianthus is in fact an escaped victim from a weapons lab. She was left out in a pile of discarded plants behind the lab, presumed to be dead. However, being exposed to the sun and rain, she recovered sufficiently to be able to crawl out through a hole under the fence and escape the impending bonfire."

Cooper soon discovered the new sample had gathered a few eccentricities – firstly her cat disappeared, leading to a sudden mouse problem which equally quickly resolved itself. A few days later upon returning home she found the Helianthus with its roots twisted around the bars of

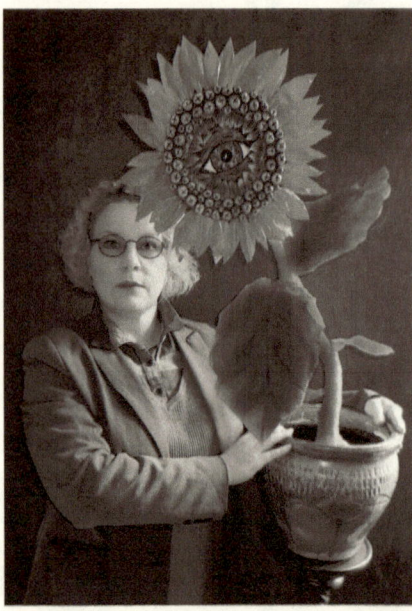

her birdcage, attempting to eat her budgerigars;

"It is my belief that the carnivorous diet that she was partial to when I first encountered her was in fact caused by the unnatural way in which she was raised and the hardships she endured after her escape. In their natural state these plants are completely benign and unthreatening."

Rather than immediately destroying the sample Cooper realised this was both a symptom of post-traumatic shock and also a signifier of a higher level of sentience than she had previously thought possible. So she did what no other human had done before – successfully provide emotional support to a plant.

"In these past months we have together managed to find a balanced diet and routine that seems more natural to the Mutant Helianthus species. She regularly gets to sit in the garden on sunny days and we have added bio fertilizer to her pot. Although mutant sunflowers are capable of moving considerable distances by what could be called extreme circumnutation, it does cause tearing and damage. This ability should probably only be considered to be a response to immediate danger and not a normal behavior."

Marit Cooper and Red Velvet are still happily living together, with a new cat and far more secure budgerigars.

See Also: Cooper, Marit.

POPPET SIMIAN

AKA: Poppet Monkey, Coffee Monkey, Voodoo Monkey

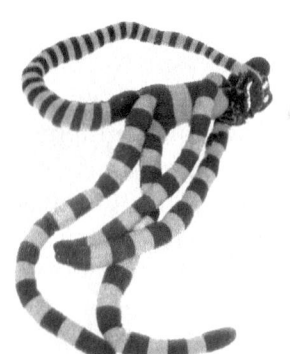

An sock monkey, usually striped, with excessively long arms and legs and a manic grin.

The first reported poppet monkey was red and black striped, and made to the pattern of a voodoo doll, or poppet, as used in sympathetic magic. All subsequent poppet monkeys have followed his method, being stitched by hand, before finding a new place to caper in.

It has been estimated that there are approximately sixty poppet simians dotted across the globe with examples being found as far away as Ohio, USA. The main concentration seems to be in central England emanating outwards, with reported sightings in Brighton, London, Cambridge and Swindon.

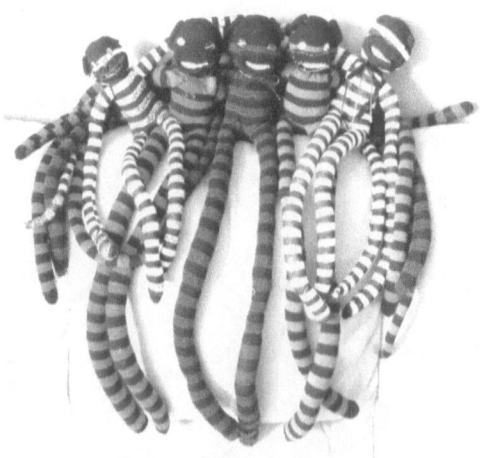

The Poppet's have been known to display particular behaviours: Ol' CM, the first known example, appeared in several adult photographic shoots and then decided to move on from his creator after an evening in the company of '…that Warn woman.' But as it's often been said; 'Monkeys don't enjoy to be cooped up in a garret'.

Ol' CM also appears as a character in Tea Time

Tales with Nonny Warn as the voice of reason who dissuades Pyrite Tannin from a life of petty thievery and teaches him to share. The poppet simians have also been seen infesting a cafe in Walsall and BIAD in Birmingham.

See Also: Nonny Warn, Pyrite Tannin

CULTS AND CULTURES

The Hkoogarlarrr

AKA: The Breathers of the Divine Breath, The Humming Tribe, The People of the Sorrowful Lament.

An ancient culture marked by constant song yet with little oral language. The practice of Hkooism involves devotion to expression through creation of art, with verbal communication being generally dedicated to poetry.

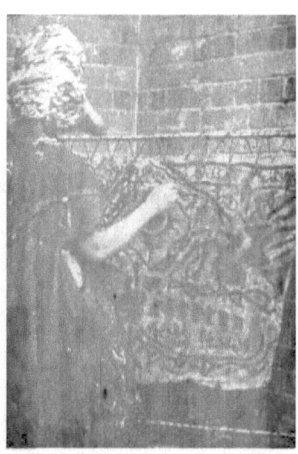

Vague reports of The Hkoogarlarrr have occurred since the seventeenth century, but their ability to seemingly evaporate into their surroundings has made any serious anthropological study impossible. Making contact with the Hkoogarlarrr was one of the reasons for the funding of the Opogo-Bunyip expedition, but it was sadly lost before it could fulfill its mission.

One of the few to actually observe the Hkoogarlarr was renowned anthropologist and historian of alternative culture Snufkin Graney Esq, whose method of transcendent anthropology enabled him to at least begin to observe this people who were shrouded in mystery and swaddled in enigma. "(I try to connect with)…the figures and peoples and

therefore cultures within these worlds. I spend my
time trying to live in their skin and environment,
see through their eyes, hear what they hear whilst
also carrying out the hum drum and monotonous
duties everyday life brings". This approach had
given Graney exceptional results in the past, and
using these methods he spent a year searching for
and six months observing the Hkoogarlarrr.

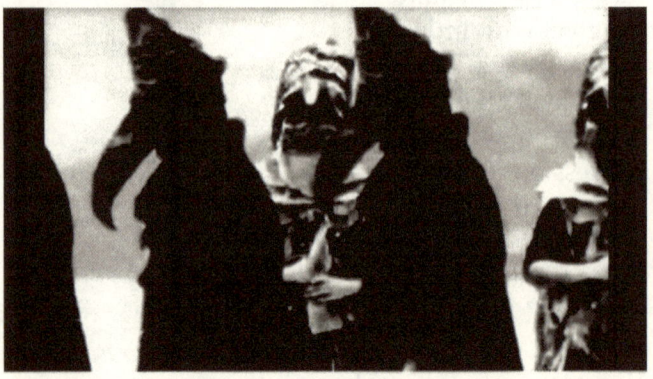

When he returned to England to present his
findings, however, he mysteriously disappeared
from his hotel room the night before his
appointment with the Broadwoodwidger Research
Institute. There was no sign of a struggle, and the
door and windows were locked and bolted from
the inside with the anthropologist not being seen
since.

Since then few further studies have been
attempted, but the footage and notes Graney
managed to acquire still form part of the Museums
collection.

See Also: Jonathan Graney, The Opogo-Bunyip Expedition

THE MONSTER'S WAGER

A.K.A: The Monster's Bargain, The Monster's Bet, The Monster's Deal

We pondered all that we had done, and all that we might be. Then it said "I'll believe in you, if you believe in me"

Full Text of the Wager, c. 2010 C.E.

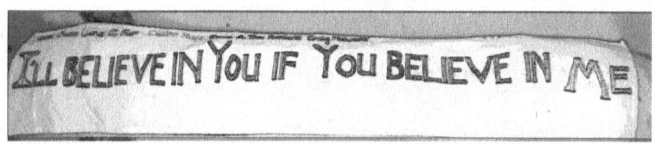

"'Do you know, I always thought Unicorns were fabulous monsters, too? I never saw one alive before!'
'Well, now that we **have** seen each other,' said the Unicorn, 'if you'll believe in me, I'll believe in you. Is that a bargain?'
'Yes, if you like,' said Alice."

Lewis Carroll's Version of the Monster's Wager, as recorded in *Through The Looking Glass and What Alice Found There*

The Monster's Wager refers to a promise of mutual belief. Usually truncated to "I'll believe in you if you believe in me" (which is essentially the promise made by participants), the deal involves a period of discourse between the participants before the agreement can be struck.

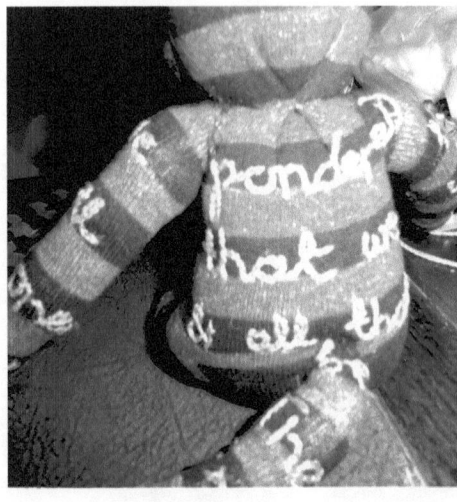

The Wager is often seem as a counter to Pascal's Wager, which suggests that belief in God is a statistically correct assumption. Nonny Warn reputedly responded to this notion by exclaiming: 'Goodness! Oh ye of little cojones! Surely everybody knows that there are lies, damned lies, and statistics!'

The Monster's Wager, like Pascal's, is simultaneously pointless and pointed, valued and worthless. By virtue of its rooting in belief, it makes it a bargain that means as much to the participants as they care for it to, without the 'you never know' underlying threat of Pascal's Bet.

See Also: 'Hail' Initiate Blind

SANCTUM MICRO COMMUNITIES

A.K.A: Mothers Burrow

Sanctum Micro Communities is an organisation

offering 'whole life management', where inhabitants enter into a facility which provides for all their needs.

SANCTUM MICRO COMMUNITIES
THE LAST DECISION YOU EVER NEED TO MAKE

"In a Sanctum Micro Community, you need never feel alone or afraid again"

Extract from SMC Advertising

Sanctum is a rather sinister organisation, offering everything a person needs to exist within a bunker shielded against biological, nuclear and natural disasters. These facilities are run entirely automatically by a Monitoring and Organisational Twin Heuristic Responder system, known as 'Mother'. This has a visual and verbal interface based on socialite, factory girl and crack-shot Kiki Casper-Jemm, although it has never been clear whether she was ever aware of her image being used in this way.

Entry to one of these communities is usually via a Pre Acceptance and Personality Assessment Application form (P.A.P.A.A.) completed at one of the company's recruitment drives. This then leads to the signing of a contract laying out the terms of residence in one of these establishments.

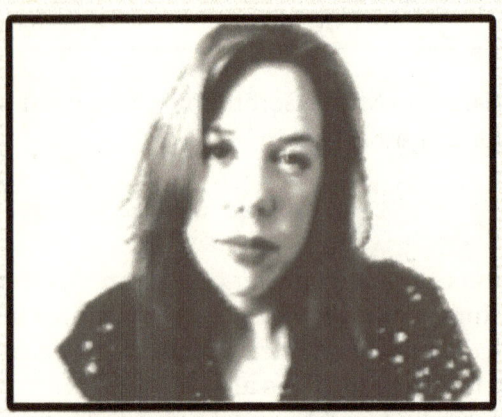

SANCTUM

MICRO COMMUNITIES

The world is a fierce and frightening place, and nobody knows what the future may hold. With the constant threat of local and international violence, the persistent worry of economic difficulties and the ongoing concern of the effects of subversive elements on your loved ones, there has never been a better time to flock to the safety of a SANCTUM MICRO COMMUNITY.

SANCTUM MICRO COMMUNITIES are designed for people like you, and every concern is provided for. A healthy diet, guaranteed employment, a safe and secure future far from the troubles of the modern world! Our modern facilities are proven to withstand Chemical, Nuclear, Biological and Natural disasters, and your health, safety and happiness are monitored constantly and engineered on a social, genetic and molecular level.

This is possible because of our breakthrough Monitoring & Organisational Twin Heuristic Empathic Responder System, or M.O.T.H.E.R.S. (affectionately known as 'Mother'). Together with ensuring the daily operations of the facility run smoothly, Mother also provides an individual interface for each inhabitant and ensures a friendly ear at any hour.

In a SANCTUM MICRO COMMUNITY,
you need never feel alone or afraid again.

The terms of these contracts are rather troubling, revealing that the company will essentially own the inhabitants, including all corporeal or non corporeal elements, that the inhabitants are required to do all suitable work assigned to them and that they will undergo any require medical examination or treatment by the company. The contract also specifies that it is Sanctum who decides what is suitable.

The appeal of such an organisation is understandable, and nobody has ever been known to leave the facility, except for those contributing to the community's promotional drives. While it is entirely possible that Sanctum is indeed a benign corporation, the lack of communication from or news about previous inhabitants is innately troubling.

See Also: Kiki Casper-Jemm

SHELLEY SMITH INDUSTRIES (S.S.I)

A.K.A Shelley Smith International, Shelley Smith Intergalactic.

A corporate entity specialising in eccentric and slightly homespun inventions.

The brainchild of eccentric C.E.O. Mister Shelley Smith, SSI was reputedly founded in a garret near Birmingham. The overpowering stench of sulphur and pleas of his landlady forced him to find larger premises, and Shelley Smith Industries gained a reputation for creating bespoke engineering and completely original design and function.

MR. SHELLEY-SMITH

No first name has ever been listed for him, but he was variously described by Tesla as 'A fine gentlemen to take sherry with' and by Edison as 'That damned Halfling'. His initial experiments into power generation were halted when it was discovered he'd been dabbling in metaphysical engineering, although this did secure him a yearly stipend partially paid by the Miskatonic University, the Broadwoodwidger research Institute and MODAD. SSI were also the firm who outfitted the ill-fated '04 Opogo-Bunyip expedition.

While he had teams of up to fifty scientists, engineers and parapsychologists working on a project at any given time, nobody else ever quite managed to either re-produce or mass-produce his inventions. As such very few examples survive, with none dating before the late nineteenth century being found.

Shelley Smith suddenly and completely withdrew from public life at some point in the 1930's – when orders went unfulfilled authorities broke into his factory to find a fully automated unit that had finally broken down – it has been estimated that the factory could have been abandoned up to five years before this discovery, and as such no exact date of disappearance can be determined. Every few years, however, a new machine is presented as a previously unknown SSI invention.

See Also: The Frozen Mole, Captain Haniver.

FIGURES AND PERSONAGES

THE ACOUSTIC STORYTELLER

A.K.A: Rich Stokes

The modern evolution of the wandering balladeer.

The Acoustic Storyteller is one on Nonny Warn's all round good eggs. It is said that she was in Monte Carlo, having just won a rather expensive bit of treasure at the roulette table at their annual Halloween Masquerade when she was approached by several rather sturdy gentlemen. She found it was becoming a rather sticky situation when a gentleman walked up, took her arm, excused them and walked Nonny to safety before her aggressors realised what had occurred.

He occasionally accompanied her while seeking treasure, but finds making rooms full of people belly-laugh infinitely more satisfying. Particularly when it's about something *slightly* wrong.

AUNTIE MABEL

AKA Kid Killer Mabel, The Wicked Schoolmistress

Manifests as a rapping sound and eerie happenings around Whitehall Junior School, Walsall.

"Auntie Mabel, In the table, Can you hear us knock?"

Old Children's Rhyme

Whitehall school was opened in the late nineteenth century in Caldmore, Walsall. According to an old school myth the first headmistress was a fearsome woman who sought to endear herself to the schools wealthy backers by promoting an image of benevolence, insisting that pupils referred to her as 'Auntie' or 'Auntie Mabel'.

However, this was an effort to disguise her abject cruelty and general hatred of children. This was primarily focused on a pupil who was a ward of the court called Charlie. Charlie wasn't reputedly bright or stupid, good or bad, but his status meant that the apparently benign 'Auntie' was asked to take care of him, which she readily agreed to.

Mabel used Charlie as her own personal slave, making him tend to the needs of the school and her household. While he did as he was told she still developed a great disdain for him and her treatment became ever more eccentric and brutal. This carried through to her treatment of the other children at the school, with corporal and psychological punishments that were considered extreme even by Victorian standards.

As Charlie approached his 11th birthday, and the end of his unofficial servitude, he began to collect evidence of Mabel's actions. When she discovered this she attacked the boy, leading to a chase up the schools bell tower where she threw the child off the tower to his death. This fracas led to the discovery of Charlie's evidence, and Mabel committed suicide in her office shortly afterwards.

Since then the ghosts of both Charlie and Mabel have been said to haunt the school, with occasional observers reporting an ethereal re-enactment of their fight on the bell tower and current pupils playing games and making dares relating to the evil 'Auntie Mabel'. Some students and a teacher held a ghost hunt at the school in the late 1980's, but no truly supernatural occurrences were reported.

CAPTAIN HANIVER

A.K.A: Capt. Erasmus Haniver, The Dread Captain, The Carny Captain

A staunch man, wild haired and eyed and keeper of 'Haniver and Son', a traveling sideshow specialising in esoteric creatures.

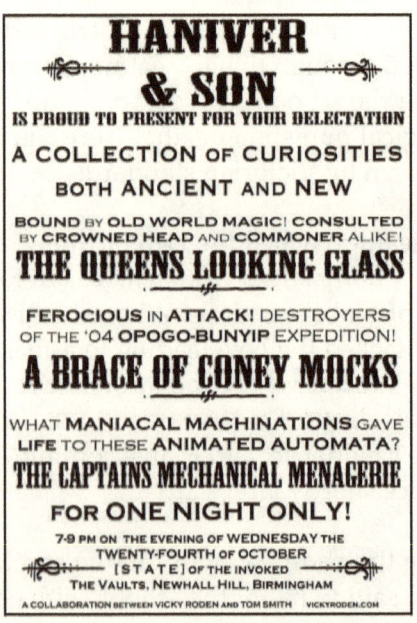

HANIVER
& SON
IS PROUD TO PRESENT FOR YOUR DELECTATION
A COLLECTION OF CURIOSITIES
BOTH ANCIENT AND NEW
BOUND BY OLD WORLD MAGIC! CONSULTED BY CROWNED HEAD AND COMMONER ALIKE!
THE QUEENS LOOKING GLASS
FEROCIOUS IN ATTACK! DESTROYERS OF THE '04 OPOGO-BUNYIP EXPEDITION!
A BRACE OF CONEY MOCKS
WHAT MANIACAL MACHINATIONS GAVE LIFE TO THESE ANIMATED AUTOMATA?
THE CAPTAINS MECHANICAL MENAGERIE
FOR ONE NIGHT ONLY!
7-9 PM ON THE EVENING OF WEDNESDAY THE TWENTY-FOURTH OF OCTOBER
[S T A T E] OF THE INVOKED
THE VAULTS, NEWHALL HILL, BIRMINGHAM
A COLLABORATION BETWEEN VICKY RODEN AND TOM SMITH   VICKYRODEN.COM

In October 2012, a thick fog descended on Birmingham, UK. It remained there for three days, unmoving. And on the third night Haniver & Son displayed a selection of their collection in a small, Victorian pub in the cities Jewelry Quarter.

Haniver displayed several key items, including the only known Coney Mocks in captivity, a variety of mechanical creatures and, two hundred years after it's first taste of fame, an enchanted looking glass. The crowd was drawn by the Captains young assistant, commonly known as Jenny or Sonny, however it seems that the title of 'Son' refers not to the Captains actual offspring (of which there are no records) but of whatever apprentice he has with him at the time.

Erasmus Haniver was at one point a real sea captain, with connections to the House of Hanover, and captained the ill-fated Opogo-Bunyip expedition. He disappeared shortly after his return after scandalously spending the night with the fiancée of another surviving member of the crew. It was after this that he first

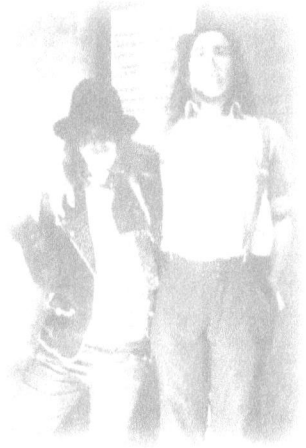

started to appear with his sideshow.

Generally operating along the coasts, Haniver's visits were always said to be preceded by fog for several days. In their heyday Haniver and Son drew crowds of several hundred visitors a day, and boasted a variety of artifacts and cryptids. This sudden popularity brought him to the attention of various authorities, and he was eventually forced to sail out to sea to escape investigation by M.O.D.A.D and legal action by Shelley Smith Industries.

Since then Haniver & Son have rarely ventured back to land, and it is not entirely clear whether the most recent appearance was that of Erasmus Haniver at all, most likely being his son or other near relative.

See Also: Coney Mocks, Shelley Smith Industries

COOPER, MARIT: See Mutant Helianthus

THE COW-PUNK GOSPEL BLUESMEN

A.K.A: Rhino and the Ranters, The Ranters, The Last Band You'll Ever See, Samedi's House Band.

Appears as a group of musicians brandishing totemistic noisemakers, led by the elegantly attired 'Doctor Rhino'

"Rhino and the Ranters are the resident band in purgatory. Their set is a blend of emotions according to the lifestyles and the final destination of their audiences. Dr Rhino steps out of the hinter realm from time to time with his band to celebrate the delights of festivals such as Dia del la motre, The Hallowed Eve, Mardi

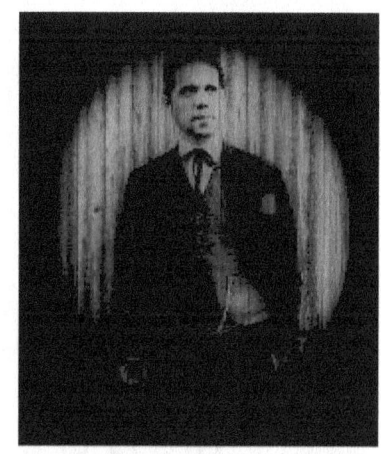

Gras and Walpurgisnacht He can be found at these times drinking rum with his friends- such notable figures as Baron Semedi and his wife Maman Brigitte, Elizabeth Device and Alice Nutter, and Aleister Crowley. But as a working musician he can always be found in the Limbo Room. Or on special occasions further down in the Inferno"

Extract from the journals of Dr. R.J. Webb

Most cultures have complex death myths, but the shadowy figure of the band playing at edge of oblivion is recurrent. In his studies into near death experiences Dr. R.J. Webb reported back after his self-experimentations that the primary memory of the whole affair was that of the house band accompanied by an overwhelming smell of rum.

The Ranters and 'Dr. Rhino' are also mentioned in

one of Nonny Warn's works:

Sooner or later you'll open your eyes,
Somewhere near your point of demise
 And find you're in the company of commoners and
kings
where the Crossroads Bodega constantly swings

This is the place where the Baron holds court
Where departures are made and extensions are bought
And, refusing to pander to pious or glum
makes your last journey special with music and rum

For no matter how dreary your earthly plight
Here it will always be Saturday Night
The clubs never empty and there's still room for more
But the Band is the biggest part of the Draw

Formed by Dr Rhino from salt, heat and smog
The ranters will always leave one agog
 There's necromancy laced with booze
at the heart of their Cow-Punk Gospel Blues

It draws from the crowd and reflects the throng
So every attendee will add to the song
Their moods resonate and their hopes crescend
To a fitting tune for their eventual end

But there are such nights, and this is one
Where Dr Rhino decides that he wants some fun
 So he brings his ranters through the veil
To teach all of us how to jive and wail.

See Also: Nonny Warn, Dr. R.J. Webb

GRANDMOTHER VIVIAN – See Merlin's Stone

GRANEY, JONATHAN – See The Hkoogarlarrr

KIKI CASPER-JEMM

A.K.A: The Black Widow, K.C. J, Casey Jay, El Presidente.

An elegant American socialite, usually attired in one of her vast collection of little black dresses.

Kiki Casper-Jemm is a resident of the Hampton's and allegedly a cousin of Nonny Warn. After studying Applied Psychology and Parapsychology at St. Jude's she spent a year (at the behest of her Grandmother Vivian) at a finishing school in Arkham, Massachusetts, which specialised in Martinis and metaphysics. While attending she was to meet her most constant friend, Mr. D'Eath, on a Women's Studies course. They dated briefly but it soon ended when both parties realised they had simultaneously been having an affair with the Head of the Faculty, Professor Maurice Fitzwilliam Penrith III, who then became Kiki's first husband.

Shortly after leaving Arkham her Grandmother Vivian died, leaving Kiki her palatial Hampton's estate. A few months later she was widowed when the Professor went sea fishing and a freak storm on a clear day caused him to get entangled in his own line. His efforts to free himself led to the line pulling tighter around his throat, partially strangling him which led him to fall overboard. Kiki was at a soiree in the company of several dozen international dignitaries at the time.

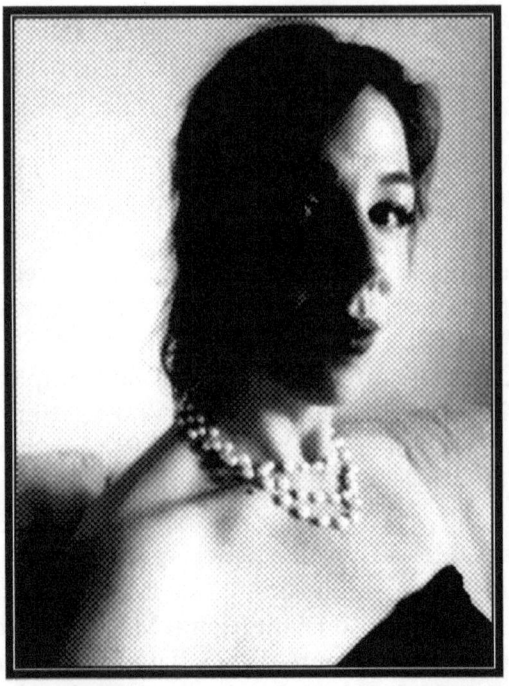

Shortly after this Kiki met her second husband, Willoughby Watson Wilkins. A confirmed bachelor til the age of 77, they met when Kiki began shooting classes and immediately embarked on a whirlwind romance involving big game hunting, shark fishing and Gin. Wilkins also assisted Kiki and Nonny Warn on several treasure hunts over the next few years and Nonny attended their wedding at the Arkham Townhouse Kiki had inherited from her first husband.

Sadly her second marriage proved even shorter than the first, with Wilkins dying on their honeymoon. The Coroner eventually relented to a verdict of natural causes, recording: "Mrs Casper-Jemm has provided us with sufficient photographic proof that the ligature marks on the body were indeed caused by sexual experimentation, borne out by the indelible satisfied grin on the face of the deceased. While it cannot be proven that any actual wrong doing has taken place, my personal opinion is that such acts (particularly on an Octogenarian) are morally, socially and ethically heinous."

The tedious gossip surrounding this led Kiki to retire from "those dull social circles" and taking something of a leave of absence. During this time she was known to have used her initials and pseudonym 'Casey Jay', and was allegedly seen associating with the Velvet Underground at Warhol's Factory, teaching Janis Joplin how to mix and appreciate "a really *fine* Martini" and speeding across the continent in a white Mustang in the company of Kerouac and Cassady. During this time she was also alleged to have had at least three further husbands.

She is now known to appear from time to time at her Hamptons Estate, usually hosting legendary parties, before disappearing again.

See Also: Nonny Warn, Grandmother Vivian

NONNY WARN

AKA: Anywn Ronn, The Dream Thief, Monster Six, That Warn Woman, El Impresaria.

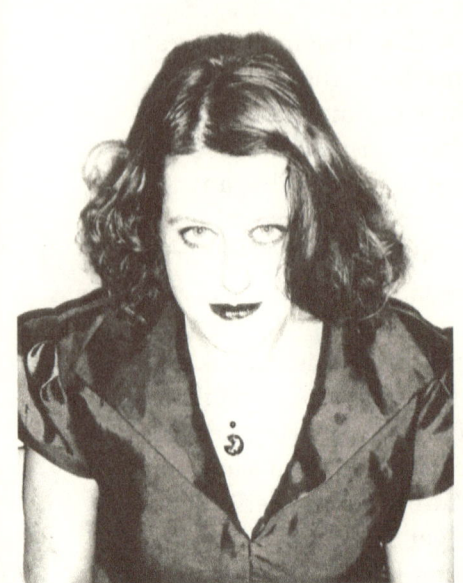

A woman of indeterminate age with curled hair, a clipped English accent and a (usually) green dress. Generally referred to as being 'differently corporeal and non-linear specific', this simply means that she can only exist in this reality at particular points and for limited times. It is said that she spends her days stepping between realities, never settling but constantly moving through a multitude of universes.

She is said to be generally charming yet at times incredibly fierce. She is said to seem terribly interested in everything, often asking myriad questions about the changes in places and taking long expeditions with her associates in search of ancient treasures. While she usually happily answers questions her answers are always suspect, and when asked why she didn't give out more details about herself replied:

"Information is a tricksy thing, one must be careful with who has it, who uses it, and must be kept guarded. I far prefer tales - they can be told to anybody, be true or false, fantasy or reality. Information cannot be distributed

freely, but tales are another story. And that is what I am - a story. A tale. A manifestation of the Monsters Wager - I'll believe in you, if you believe in me."

Nonny Warn is a teller of tales and dispenser of stories. There are examples of characters that could be her scattered across history, normally a stranger who arrives during turbulent times and uses a mixture of charm, wit and scandalous behaviour to get by.

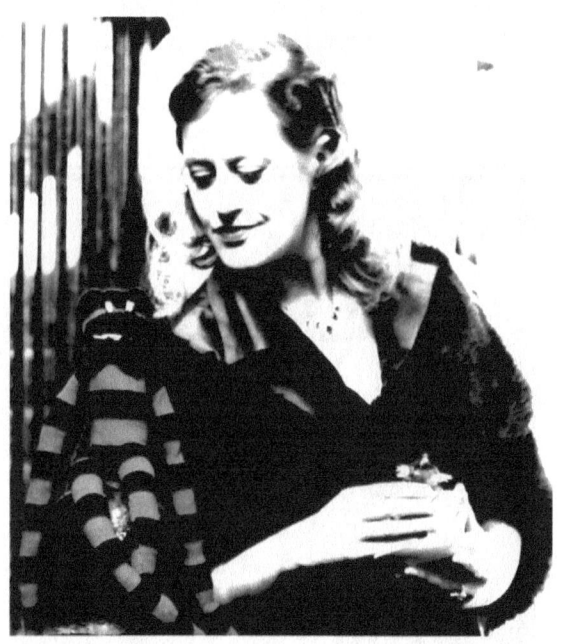

She has been known to associate with several figures including Kiki Casper-Jemm, whom she refers to as 'cousin' and has been a regular attendee at her weddings. She has also been linked with Dr Rhino and has been 'romantically' linked with Mr.

Shelley-Smith and Nikolai Alexandroff, the sell-sword-for-vodka.

There have been a number of confirmed sightings of Warn, and she does tend to leave definite records of her existence – the series of stories known as 'Tea Time Tales', ephemera from events such as 'A Walpurgis Night of Vaudeville' and notes, artifacts and instructions signed with a letter N and a kiss. Such notes and references have shown up in the Broadwoodwidger Archive, among the personal effects of deceased dignitaries and at least once in the records of Hansard.

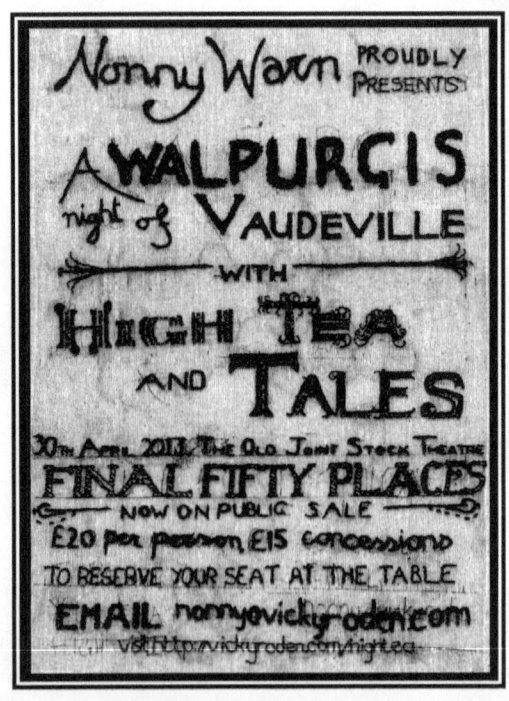

Another significant aspect of the Nonny Warn myth is her policy of non-interference. She claims to have guidelines she follows when in a new place, namely showing some decorum, taking the time to make friends and most importantly of all:

"Don't interfere. A lesson learned the hard way, but intervention is rarely a good plan. I observe, and sometimes advise. But it's a bad show to intervene. Because when you do that you take control, and it's not your world to rule."

There has been a definite pattern to reported sightings of Warn. She normally manifests for several occasions within days of each other for a period of up to three weeks, before seeming to evaporate. There have also been historical references to her dating back to the nineteenth century, almost entirely connected with stories, myth or legend in some way.

There has been a marked increase in frequency in reports of Nonny Warn, but a theory has been mooted that this is in fact due to the vast improvements in and portability of technology. This is supported by one particular note, found in 1972 by Miss J Cook in her great-uncles safe when executor of his estate. The note read 'Darling, I brought this too early, be a dear and keep hold of it til I can pop back. Love, N x.' The envelope also contained a small chip of what seemed to be class. It took forty years for the technology to read the chip to be developed and was found to hold a recording of a woman who is unmistakably Nonny Warn. The dates and events she refers to have not yet occurred, but when challenged about this she smiled and said "dear, it's just another tale for another day"

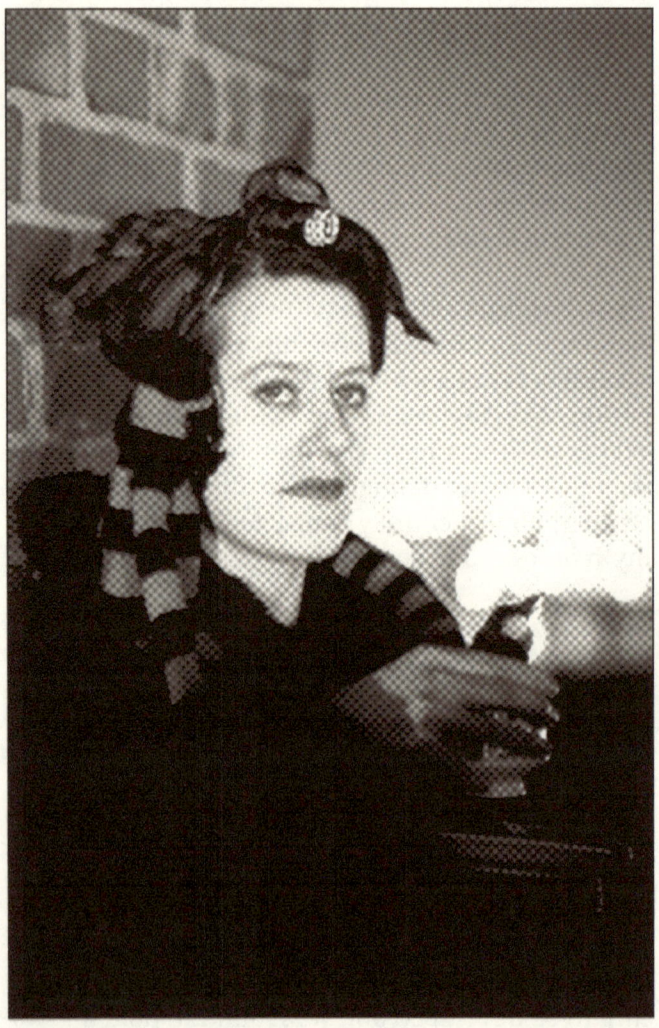

The majority of Nonny's most recent appearances have been in the Midlands. She has been observed telling tales in art galleries, making grown men and women form a crocodile while on walks, yelling at diners to make more noise with their soup and on Walpurgisnacht 2013 hosting a grand soiree involving cake and visits from her 'all round good eggs'. 'High Tea and Tales – A Walpurgis night of Vaudeville' included Dr. Rhino, the Fallen Angel, The Swinging Singing showgirl, The Wandering Balladeer, the Acoustic Storyteller and the Rat-Pack Escapee together with communications with Kiki Casper-Jemm and an unexpected visit from The Queen of the May.

While very little has been written about Warn herself there is one poem that is widely regarded to relate to her origins:

There once was a girl, she needs no name.
Such creatures often seem the same
But she lived her life from day-to-day
And went out to learn, and went out to play.

She knew little pain and she knew less strife
In her neat and tidy, organised life
But as she grew older she started to dream
On an ancient, eerie and mystical theme.

She sought out old tomes in forgotten words
In tongues no living ears could have heard
She travelled so far to continue these frolics
In the hallowed halls of the Miskatonic

She faced great danger and took such risks

To poke the mysteries of the universe with sticks
She rode on the gift horse and tore out its tooth
And checked her reflection in the fountain of youth

She danced with the Dryads and drank mead with Pan,
Rescued great treasures from terrible clans
Returned an old ring to where Rhine maidens swirled
But, for all that, remained just a girl.

A girl who still lived day after day
Stuck to a single temporal plane
A girl who saw hints of metaphysical doors
Where few had braved to venture before

For this girl had a secret, terrible fear
And every adventure made it more clear
That it wouldn't be very long before
There were no more mysteries left to explore.

She knew of a means to open those doors
Through which so few had ventured before.
Knew she could take little more than the things she had
learned
And that travellers rarely, if ever, returned.

So, dressed in her finest and consciously neat
(For one never quite knows just whom one might meet)
She slipped through the gap at realities end
Fully prepared to meet foe or meet friend.

Now it wouldn't be proper, and wouldn't be fair
To reveal exactly what this girl found there
Though she did make a deal with each creature she'd see
And promised 'I'll believe in you, if you believe in me'

And so she endures, to this very day
Though in what time or place no one can say
But she still flits through the strange and the real
Inviting all creatures to join in her deal.

Indeed, Nonny Warn is the focus of two particular legends. The first is that of the Monsters Wager, which Nonny Warn is reported to strike with all those she meets, and also that of the dream thief in the legends surrounding the Blade of the Red Valley. She has certainly been quoted as saying "If you make such Humdrum use of your imagination you shan't be allowed to keep it".

There is no reference to the corporeal existence of anyone by the name of Nonny Warn in the birth or death records of any country. However there was a student who frequently visited the Broadwoodwidger Museum and received a scholarship to the Miskatonic in the early 1930's by the name of Anwyn Ronn. Miss Ronn reputedly disappeared on a field trip with no trace of her remains ever being found. There are some who, due to the style of Nonny's clothing and decided anachronism together with her constant seeking of treasure, consider this to have been Anwyn's ultimate fate.

There is, however, the possibility that she is merely a crazy lady in a green dress.

PYRITE TANNIN

Menace of the Seven Seas (formerly), Monster Twelve.

A fat-bellied man wearing a brown three-cornered hat, a light and dark blue banded jersey, dark blue and black pinstriped trousers and yellow wellington boots. He also sports a long grey beard and has a false front tooth made of iron pyrite. Often depicted with a cup and teapot, his colours consist of the cup-and-crossed-spoons and Tannin is the subject of the tale 'The Treasure Hunt of Pyrite Tannin' by Nonny Warn.

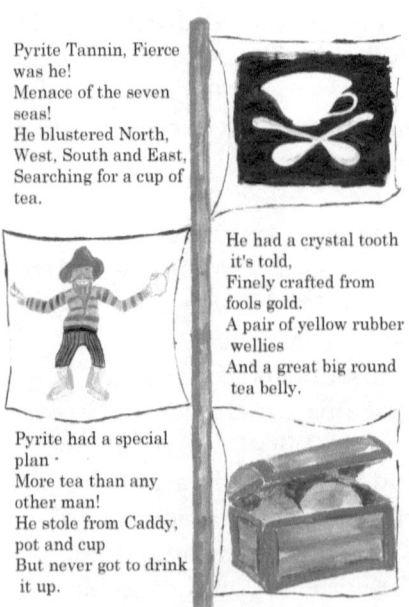

Pyrite Tannin, Fierce was he!
Menace of the seven seas!
He blustered North, West, South and East,
Searching for a cup of tea.

He had a crystal tooth it's told,
Finely crafted from fools gold.
A pair of yellow rubber wellies
And a great big round tea belly.

Pyrite had a special plan ·
More tea than any other man!
He stole from Caddy, pot and cup
But never got to drink it up.

Formerly a 'Ruffian of the Sea' with designs on the entire planets tea supply, Tannin is now a reformed character who seeks thirsty travellers on the ocean and invites them to share his brew, returning to land (and his visitors to their boats) only when he has exhausted his supplies of drinking water. He is usually to be found on the waves, and only lingers on land when depressed or dejected.

See Also: Nonny Warn, The Thirteen Monsters, Poppet Simians (Ol' CM).

THE RAT PACK ESCAPEE

AKA: Craig Howard

Every so often, everybody needs a little inspiration. The tale of this obscure character is referenced in this tale:

Now, Frank was a frightfully talented chap,
A voice to be reckoned with, but for all that
He sometimes was shy, and sometimes was blue
This fellow certainly needed a muse!

So one was packed off, and met with the fellow
Showed him how to sing swinging and mellow
And, upon meeting the creatures that Frank named as friends
Suggested a group show might meet their ends

So Frank and his fellows had the world at their feet
But frank could be jealous in the LA Heat
And grew concerned that the muse who'd been so quick to help
Might become the star of the show himself

This muse had nothing like that on his mind
But was as ever helpful and kind
And had arranged his time so he could spend
A day at Ava and Laurens's spa weekend

Frank got cross at this, and how!

Is this what his muse was doing now?
Spending time with Frank's favourite dames,
Not on your life! Frank proclaimed.

On his return from a thoroughly relaxing break
With Ava and Lauren giggling away
Frank, accusing him of all manner of wrong
Finally offended this muse of song

Frank threw a punch, and the muse stepped away.
Frank failed to land a single blow that day.
The muse simply ducked, and with great panache
Threw a right hook that landed blue eyes on his ass

The muse then decided to take his leave,
Before Frank woke up, and felt all aggrieved
So Now Mr. Howard can freely sing
Without carrying a follower under his wing

MR. Shelley-Smith: **See Shelley Smith Industries**

The Swinging Singing Showgirl

AKA: Bexi Owen, The Land-Siren.

Manifests as a young female human, usually a singer although quite often dances.

This tale has been often mistaken as a variation on

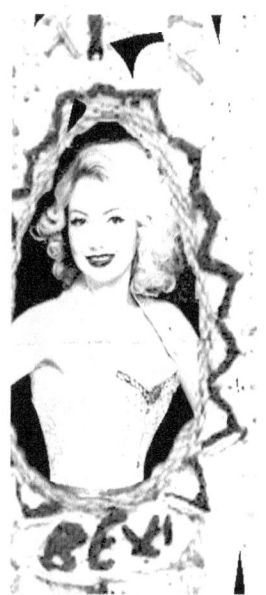 Hans Christian Andersons 'The Little Mermaid', but variations of it have cropped up across Europe, with the earliest being linked to later Greek mythology. The tale speaks of a Siren who, bored with the monotony of luring seamen to their deaths, seeks to sing in a place she can do no harm. When she reaches land she finds those who hear her still become mortally entranced. In some versions she drowns herself, unable to return to the sea – however, this 'Nonny Warn' fable suggests an eventual happier ending for her:

In days of Yore such tales were told
Of Sailors young and strong and bold
Whose journeys ended in the hold
Of the Sirens Song

The siren thought it quite a bore,
 Having seen such things before
And so she thought it might be grand
 To hear her song echo on land

So on Land she walked until she'd got
 To the most acoustically suitable spot
And soon people gathered to this plot
To Hear the Faery's song

But time moves on, and so does she
With infinite places she could be
And has been – she now commands
 Top Billing in a hundred lands!

Now men and women everywhere
Dress in their best and primp their hair
And warm the edges of their chairs
To see the Showgirls Song

At the recently reported Walpurgisnacht
disturbance in Birmingham, one of the performers
was indeed a showgirl who went by the name of
Bexi Owen.

THE SIXTH VISCOUNT OF BROADWOODWIDGER

A.K.A: Charlton Amhurst

"Haude Scientia Est Inconcessus" (No Knowledge is
Forbidden)
                          Broadwoodwidger Family Motto

Charlton Amhurst, the Sixth Viscount of
Broadwoodwidger was a renowned collector of

curiosities, Fellow of the Miskatonic University and bachelor. He founded the museum which still bears his name in the early part of the nineteenth century when he sought to ensure the preservation of his collection and continuation of his research when he went to fight in the later part of the Napoleonic Wars.

He did this by establishing the 'Broadwoodwidger Museum of Cryptozoology and Mythology' at his town lodgings in Liskeard and bestowing a healthy endowment to fund its ongoing maintenance. Over the next few years the institution attracted visitors and researchers from across the country, and upon his return he was so impressed by the reputation the museum had gained that he established it as a more permanent centre for the research of the mythological and public display of unusual and inexplicable objects.

Amhurst was considered something of an eccentric, firstly when he refused to follow the family tradition of a place at Cambridge and went to the United States. Not to visit, or look at the Native Americans, or even sow his wild oats, but to study at the recently founded Miskatonic at Arkham, Massachusetts. His choice of an American institution reportedly caused great consternation in society, but not to his family, unlike his alleged relationship with Vivian Casper-Jemm who was barely sixteen.

The other area of Amhurst's eccentricity focused on his areas of research – particularly those he was engaged in during his military career. All notes from this period are simply marked as 'Lost' on the museums ledgers, but it's believed that the work he carried out between 1811 and 1820 was the beginnings of M.O.D.A.D.

The Amhurst family continues to remain the custodians of the Broadwoodwidger Museum, which recently celebrated in Bi-Centenary.

THE WANDERING BALLADEER

A.K.A: The First Storyteller, Claire Mace.

From the research notes of Anwyn Ronn, Broadwoodwidger Research Institute c. 1933

"There used to be scores of such people, roaming from place to place, learning songs in each village and recanting them wherever they went. This is how tales first travelled.

This particular balladeer first held my ear when I was a girl - I was entranced by her haunting voice and her seemingly endless stream of songs. Then I kept seeing her, peering out of old books and in the background of centuries old paintings, always unchanging as if she stepped between eras as easily as walking from room to room. It was her example which pointed out my own path and served as a starting point to my own fascinations with stories and such mysteries as a reality is made of.

But I've always considered her to be a force of nature, a spirit whose soul is composed of the songs we pour into her. She will exist as long as there are songs to sing, and

*there will be songs to sing as long are there are ears to
her them."*

See Also: Nonny Warn

WEBB, DR. R.J. See The Cow Punk Gospel Bluesmen

OBJECTS AND ITEMS

THE BLADE OF THE RED VALLEY

A.K.A: The Dreamstealer, The Elf-Blade, Tell-Tales-Ruin

A ruby, approximately the size of a bean, cut to an edge and set into a silver ring.

The 'Blade of the Red Valley' was originally

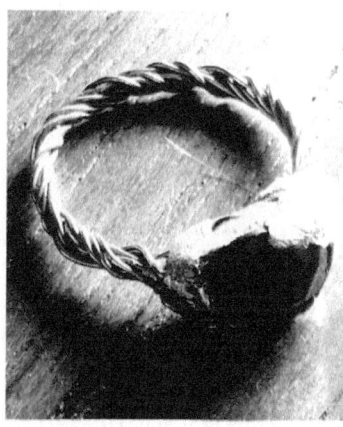

considered to be little more than an ancestral jewel of the Roden family. It was said that back in less civilised times a warring family attempted to sack the Roden homestead and the youngest daughter defended he rself against her attackers by slashing at them with the broken edge of a glass gem, mortally wounding two and surviving until help came. Her father had a ruby cut in the same manner and set in silver to commemorate the event, with the gem being passed to the youngest daughter in the family on the owner's death.

The ring was lost in the late 1940's when Adrienne Roden bet it on black at Monte Carlo. Nonny Warn bet red.

The colourful names attributed to the item relate to

several stories which have two common elements –
a ring used a blade, or to in some way pierce or cut
the victim, and the subsequent removal of the
victims soul, spirit, or in some examples their
imaginations. One such example is children rhyme
the 'Tell-Tales-Ruin':

Little boys race and little girls run
 For if you tell tales then Nonny may come

She hunts down the stories and tables the words
 And carefully notes down each name that occurs

She finds the tale-teller and pierces their head
Slits through the mind with the bright blade of red

Pulls out the fables and winds in the yarns
Then shuts the mind tight using one of her charms

And once all the fancies are stripped from the brain
They'll never tell tall tales or stories again

The Tell-Tales-Ruin, c.1910

In such stories the ruby often changes hue, from a
'pale and watery crimson' to a such a dark red that
'…only the hypnotising red flashes told as to its
true colour.' Usually the narrative is a warning to
tellers of both tall and tawdry tales – 'if you make
such humdrum use of your imagination then you
shan't be allowed to keep it' – but the central
character has also been represented as acting
kindly towards those suffering nightmares by
taking their ability to dream away.

See Also: Nonny Warn

THE GILDED KITTEN

AKA: The Cat-Ladies Totem, The Ailurophile Fetish, The Golden Pussy

A Small, Golden effigy of a cat with inlaid Jet eyes.

The Gilded Kitten is an odd object – references to it have been found from the early eighteenth century, but it has no stylistic roots in any major culture. In all reports it is an object of obsession, often driving those who own it to madness of one form or another.

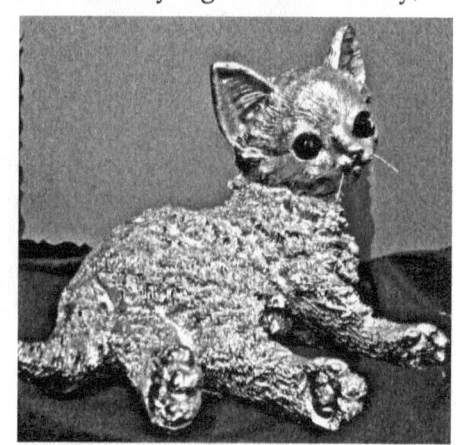

The first report of the creature involves a young noblewoman who, while visiting a curiosity shop on the continent, saw the item and asked its price. The shopkeeper replied that it wasn't for sale, so she continued to return each day, offering a larger and larger price for the ornament.

On the final day, when about to return to England, she visited the shop wearing her simplest outfit and delivered her trunks and luggage to the shop, declaring, "This is everything I own. I wish to return home in the clothes I stand in, and with that creature, and you can have everything else". The shopkeeper accepted these terms, but warned her that the object had a tendency to find itself new owners, and she would know when that time came.

Upon her return home the Gilded Kitten became a talking point of her house, and she also started to feed all the local felines, going so far as to visit local towns and bring strays home. Never marrying, she became a recluse for several years. Then one day, quite out of the blue, she was discovered aimlessly wandering around the village saying, "It's gone, and they've gone, and oh, I do so want it back!" The statue had vanished, probably stolen by a much-beleaguered member of staff, and she died (apparently of a broken heart) a few days later.

The Gilded Kitten seemed to disappear but was then mentioned in the personal effects of Louis Wain c.1939, and was reportedly hunted by avid collector of occult and obscure relics Hitler for its reputed mesmerising powers. It eventually and mysteriously delivered to the vaults of the Broadwoodwidger Museum on Walpurgisnacht 1946 with note that simply read 'I trust you know how to deal with this bad kitty. Take care dear ones, N. x'

Recently, while attempting to photograph the item for this compendium, it was discovered that images of the item seem to be undeletable. First snapped on a Smartphone, the photograph seemed to corrupt its memory and somehow managed to set itself as wallpaper, lock screen and screensaver, and all attempts to wipe it off the system proved useless. Similarly while photographing exhibits with a digital camera the photograph refused to allow itself to be permanently deleted – as such the Gilded Kitten now resides in a restricted area of the museum.

'HAIL' INITIATE BLIND

AKA: The Novice's Blinkers

A clay mask and blindfold, marked in cuneiform.

Little is known about the uses of this object. Although ostensibly ancient in design, the Italian influenced shaping and English translation of the Cuneiform markings belie its more modern origins.

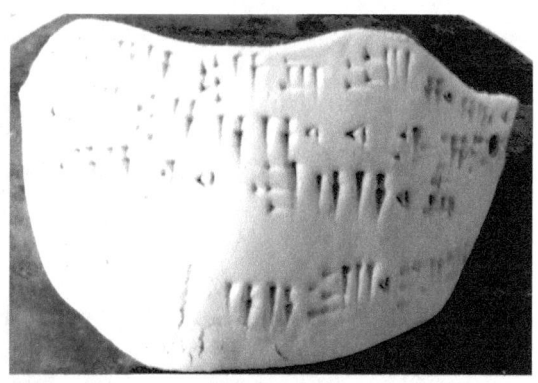

The mask is marked on both sides, with the outer lettering translating as 'I always thought you were a fabulous creature' and the inner being a variant of the Monsters Wager. This suggests that, while the Wager was generally taken in a light hearted manner, there were those who applied levels of ritual and ceremony to its undertaking.

See Also: The Monster's Wager

THE HAND OF GLORY

A small, desiccated arm including hand and shoulder.

Traditionally a hand of glory is a magical object, a five-tapered candle made from the arm of a hanged man, variously cut down or prepared at midnight, or under a full moon, or a new one. When lit this bestowed invisibility on the holder while ensuring all sleeping in the building remained asleep making it a metaphysical must for burglars hand housebreakers.

In Walsall, UK, it refers to a local legend attributed to a severed arm found in a local pub. In the late nineteenth century an arm and an English Civil War sword were found together in the attic of the White Hart pub, and while the sword became lost to the annals of history the arm was kept. The tale goes that a group of thieves were meeting in the White Hart's attic, planning their next misadventure. They were apparently overheard by one of the kitchen girls, who crept up to the attic to spy on them. She was discovered and murdered by the panicking brigands, who were then caught trying to move her body in several pieces from the pub.
She is still said to haunt the building, but no sign of her has ever occurred on several ghost hunts, and the building has since been converted into flats

with none of the tenants complaining about unwarranted bumps in the night.

The Hand of Glory has since been on continuous display at the Walsall Museum, originally in a glass case but now in a far more disappointingly child friendly format.

THE IVORY SCYTHE

A.K.A: Husbands Bane

An Exquisitely designed scythe, with an ebony handle inlaid with mother of pearl, Dodo's teeth and anointed with the tears of unicorns. The blade is reputedly carved from a Sasquatch Femur, but is more likely to be an especially fine variety of ivory.

According to legend the blade was created by a highly accomplished woman who wished to be freed from the marriage her father had arranged for her. Death himself heard of its beauty and power, as nothing was immune to it, and asked her what she would like in return for it. She explained her problematic marriage and a deal was struck – the owner of the blade would be able to call on Death to deal with such specific problems, and Death could always borrow it for special occasions, reaping fey folk and parties.

See Also: Kiki Casper-Jemm

MERLIN'S STONE

A.K.A: Merlin's Gaol, The Fairies Door.

Merlin (of Arthurian fame) reputedly fell in love with a nymph, or a kings daughter, called Niamh or Vivian or Nimue. She rejected his advances, demanding that her teach her everything he knew. The besotted old wizard agreed, and some time later the girl used her skills to trap her potential suitor in a stone.

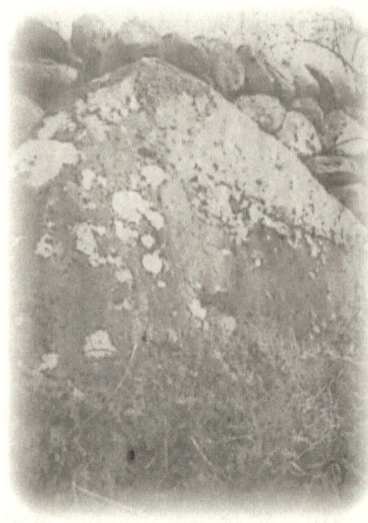

Reports of the ultimate success vary, with some saying he quickly escaped (but got the message) and others saying that he lingers there still.

There is a large, odd stone in a wall in the campsite at Nantcol Falls in Gwynedd, Wales. It sticks out and seems alien to the stones around it, and has been suggested by some as being the stone where Merlin was trapped. Strange phenomena have been observed in this area – odd periods of calm weather while surrounding areas are stormy, strange behaviour in both livestock and wildlife – and visitors have reported receiving electric shocks from the rock.

A team from the Broadwoodwidger Museum of

Cryptozoology and Mythology investigated the stone in the early 20th century, but never published their findings.

A.K.A: The Magic Mirror, The Dirty Mirror

In 1812 The Brothers Grimm published their first collection of folk tales, including Snow White. The Mirror consulted by the queen in that story became an overnight celebrity, in huge demand at society parties, lecture tours and cabinet meetings for the next few decades. At it's most popular it was polished hourly by a team of virgins with dusters of swan's feathers and cloths of silk, using rare extracts from various marine mammals.

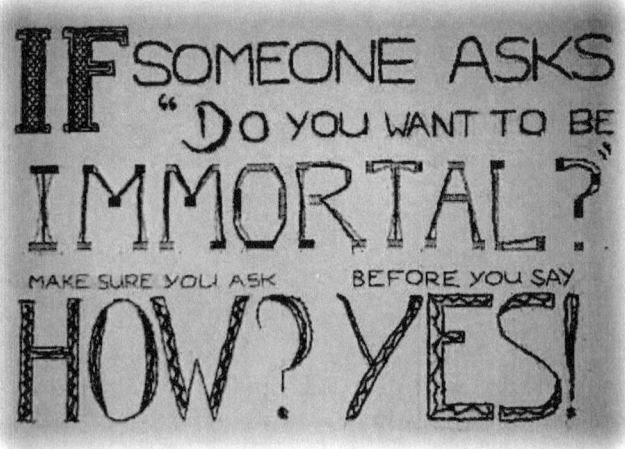

IF SOMEONE ASKS "DO YOU WANT TO BE IMMORTAL?" MAKE SURE YOU ASK HOW? BEFORE YOU SAY YES!

Fame, however, is fickle, and the mirror was 'obtained' by P.T. Barnum and subsequently 'liberated' by Capt. Erasmus Haniver for his eternally traveling sideshow 'Haniver & Son'. The creation of the mirror is allegedly an Old World Soul spell involving a closed portal which traps the victim. The soul in the mirror was allegedly that of the cleverest man alive who was offered eternal life by a Necromancer in the late seventeenth century.

Unfortunately the man's hopes of an eternity of study and contemplation were dashed when he was spellbound to the glass and packed off to Bavaria as a Royal Wedding present. As the mirror would later lament; "If someone offers to make you immortal, make sure you ask HOW before you say YES!"

The last appearance of the Glass in public showed it as being, (rather than the benign dispenser of truth portrayed in the tale) coarse and foul mouthed, a girl who asked how to be rich was advised to 'Get into whoring but stay out of crack' and it spent a good deal of the night screaming at Haniver's Son for it's fix of Windowline.

Since then The Queens Looking Glass has apparently been acquired by Nonny Warn, as the Captain now refuses to be seen with it in public.

See Also: The Necromancer, Erasmus Haniver.

THE STIPPLERS SCRY

AKA: The Character Clock, The Monster Diviner

A Stipplers Scry generally appears to be a clock or watch with thirteen numbers and twenty-six names.

There's very little information as to the exact use of the scry. First recorded examples were merely considered indicative of a slightly different time system, but the tendency of such timepieces, regardless of their state of repair, to change position seemingly at will led to further investigation. However despite the best efforts of various metaphysical researchers the Scry remains a mystery – while it does seem to be a device for telling who, and what, and when, it's exact functions are still very much of an enigma and the scry seems to function more as an indicator rather than a means of divination.

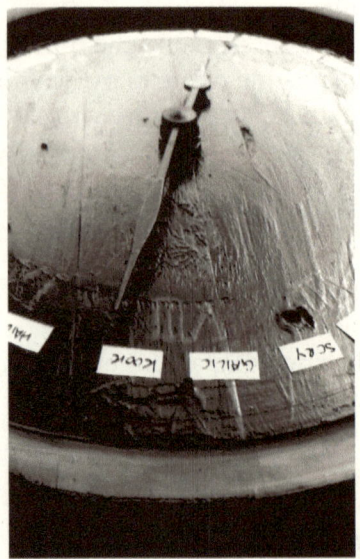

FANATICAL FANTASY, THE MYTH AND THE MAN

THE HON. MISS CECELIA AMHURST, HEAD OF THE BOARD
OF TRUSTEES, BROADWOODWIDGER MUSEUM

I quite often take a cup of Earl Grey Tea in the evening. And each time I do I imagine the voice of Captain Jean-Luc Picard of the Starship Enterprise demanding "Tea. Earl Grey. Hot." Many other fans of Star Trek – The Next Generation can claim the same, and it serves to illustrate a lovely point; that fantasies and myths serve to enhance the tapestry of our lives. They leave little snatches of dialogue that act as an accompanying tune to the everyday, little memories that make us smile when there's no one else around.

I chose this example from among the seemingly limitless alternatives as Star Trek itself has emerged from the realms of fantasy to become mythological. So much so that a recent 'reboot' of the franchise in the cinema immediately established itself as being part of another favourite science fiction staple, the parallel universe, in order to neatly sidestep the inevitable complaints about deviation from established lore. This is not the same reality. By accepting this, the viewer also unknowingly acknowledges (if only for the duration of the film) that the previously established TV shows, films and books are a reality of their own.

A great deal of this only possible because of the sheer devotion of the shows fans - Star Trek was one of the first television programs to inspire such activities as fan art and fan fiction, due in part to the cancellation of the series four years into its 'five year mission', leading to vast speculation as to the events of that final year.

It was the existence of these fans that convinced

Paramount Pictures that there would be an audience for a Star Trek film, and their continued fervour and lust for new tales from this world supported the development of several more films and the related series' of 'The Next Generation', 'Deep Space Nine' and 'Voyager'. The sheer amount of material relating to this world and the vast variety of forms it takes (including films, games, records, technical guides, fiction and artworks) suggests not a disparate rabble of admirers but a functioning community with this as its shared heritage. Just as one may feel a sense of patriotism when considering the achievements of a countryman, here there is a feeling of kinship through this uniting, albeit fantastic, mythology.

Since my fifth Great-Grandfather established the museum the family has taken its continued upkeep very seriously, with my father making the sixth generation to ensure its continuation. The old family motto is 'Haude Scientia Est Inconcessus', translating as either 'No knowledge is forbidden' or 'No science is prohibited', and the desire that all our resources are available freely to any who might seek them has been a cornerstone of the institution from the beginning. Like the fans of Star Trek, I also feel a sense of kinship through mythology, a feeling of fraternity with those who spent time working or researching at the museum. They are all with me on the shared journey to ensure that no knowledge is ever forbidden, and have all been part of the mythology commonly known as reputation which the museum has achieved in its two hundred year history. We hope to continue to preserve and discern the fantasies of the past to better appreciate the mythologies of our future.

INDEX

ABOUT THE COMPENDIUM

Written by Vicky Roden
With contributions by:
Jana K. Cook
Marit Cooper
Jonathan Charles Graney
Ian Messenger
Thomas S. Smith

More information about the project and the artist is
available at
rodenscompendium.wordpress.com
&
vickyroden.com